TOUGH TRIVIA
for Kids

OFFICIAL MENSA PUZZLE BOOK

HELENE HOVANEC

Sterling Publishing Co., Inc.
New York

10   9   8   7   6   5   4   3   2

Published by Sterling Publishing Co., Inc.
387 Park Avenue South, New York, NY 10016
© 2005 by Helene Hovanec
Distributed in Canada by Sterling Publishing
c/o Canadian Manda Group, 165 Dufferin Street
Toronto, Ontario, Canada M6K 3H6
Distributed in Great Britain and Europe by Chris Lloyd at Orca Book
Services, Stanley House, Fleets Lane, Poole BH15 3AJ, England
Distributed in Australia by Capricorn Link (Australia) Pty. Ltd.
P.O. Box 704, Windsor, NSW 2756, Australia

Sterling ISBN 1-4027-2136-6

For information about custom editions, special sales, premium and
corporate purchases, please contact Sterling Special Sales
Department at 800-805-5489 or specialsales@sterlingpub.com.

CONTENTS

Introduction 5

Quadruples 7

Two for One 19

Relations 32

Singles 46

Answers 81

Index 94

About the Author

Helene Hovanec has been hooked on puzzles
and word games since she was six years old.
She is the author of more than 45 puzzle books.

Helene Hovanec puzzle books, published by Sterling

Around the World in 80 Puzzles
Chrisscross Puzzles for Kids
The Incredible Science Puzzle Challenge
Sit & Solve Crisscross Puzzles
Stopwatch Puzzles
Tough Trivia for Kids
My First Puzzles: Easy First Puzzles
My First Puzzles: I Can Read Puzzles

Introduction

- What sandwich cookie is found in Cookies 'n Cream ice cream?
- What summer month has no major holidays?
- How many days are in a fortnight?
- Which Australian critters live on eucalyptus leaves?

These are a few of the questions you will find inside this book. A trivia quiz is a way for you to test your knowledge of a variety of subjects—everything from art to music to sports to food, with many other categories in-between. If you've never tried a trivia quiz before, this could be the beginning of a great new hobby, one that will help you learn a little bit about a lot of different stuff.

The answers are in order at the back of the book, but you don't have to go back and forth with every question. Write out or circle multiple-choice answers on the page or grab a scrap of paper to put down your answers, then go to the answer section at the back of the book to see how you did. What's great about trivia quizzes is, even if your answer is wrong, you come out ahead because you learned something.

Most important of all, have fun!

Quadruples

Circle the right answer for each question.

1. Which scale is used to measure the strength of earthquakes?

Doppler
Celsius
Richter
Fahrenheit

2. Dr. Jonas Salk invented a vaccine to wipe out what disease?

Diphtheria
Yellow fever
Polio
Mumps

3. Sam-I-am is a character in which Dr. Seuss book?

The Cat in the Hat
Green Eggs and Ham
Horton Hatches the Egg
If I Ran the Circus

4. What do the initials USC stand for?

University of Spoiled Children
University of South Carolina
University of Southern Connecticut
University of Southern California

5. The Magnolia State is the nickname for:

Mississippi
Montana
Maryland
Maine

6. What was the world's tallest building in 1931?

John Hancock Center
Empire State Building
Petronas Tower
World Trade Center

7. Which musical instrument is NOT a woodwind?

Xylophone
Oboe
Piccolo
Clarinet

8. Which color is a shade of red?

> Cardinal
> Topaz
> Sapphire
> Marigold

9. "Mad" cow disease destroys which part of a cow?

> Small intestine
> Liver
> Brain
> Heart

10. What is the largest city in Australia?

> Darwin
> Sydney
> Alice Springs
> Adelaide

11. What is the last letter in the Greek alphabet?

> Zeta
> Omega
> Alpha
> Upsilon

12. Which English scientist was the first to understand the law of gravity?

Stephen Hawking
Galileo Galilei
Johannes Kepler
Isaac Newton

13. The snack food "ants on a log" is usually made with which crunchy veggie?

Corn
Carrot
Celery
Cucumber

14. An andiron that supports logs in a fireplace is also known as a:

Fireball
Firedog
Firetrap
Firecracker

15. Which President's face is NOT on Mount Rushmore?

Jimmy Carter
Abraham Lincoln
George Washington
Thomas Jefferson

16. Which of the following best describes the Underground Railroad?

> The subway system in New York City
> A safe network to help slaves escape to freedom during the Civil War
> The Metro system in Washington, D.C.
> One of the cards on a Monopoly board

17. The English Channel is:

> A body of water between England and Ireland
> A body of water between England and France
> Another name for the British Broadcasting Corporation (BBC)
> A cable station showing only British comedies

18. Which hero from children's literature traveled to a land called Lilliput where all the residents were six inches tall?

> Stuart Little
> Sir Galahad
> Gulliver
> Captain Hook

19. Tourists in which city often take a ride in a gondola, a kind of long, narrow boat?

Vienna
Venezuela
Vancouver
Venice

20. Musician/author Daniel Handler is better known as:

Harry Potter
Ricky Martin
Lemony Snicket
Lil' Romeo

21. Which major league basketball team is based in Los Angeles?

Celtics
Warriors
Lakers
Nuggets

22. Which "ism" means copying someone else's work and passing it off as your own?

Absenteeism
Plagiarism
Quackism
Criticism

23. Which meat is usually NOT found on pizza?

Kielbasa
Sausage
Meatballs
Pepperoni

24. Which term describes a delicate situation?

Touch and go
Touch me not
Touch football
Touchy-feely

25. Which two European countries occupy the Iberian Peninsula?

France and Germany
Spain and Portugal
Greece and Turkey
Czech Republic and Slovakia

26. Which showman and circus founder is famous for these words: "There's a sucker born every minute"?

Buffalo Bill
Nick Carter
Tom Hanks
P.T. Barnum

27. Which movie star/comedian was known as the Little Tramp?

> Charles Bronson
> Charlie Chaplin
> Charlie Brown
> Prince Charles

28. Hydrology is the study of:

> Hydrogen
> Human cultures
> Water
> Plants

29. Which American outlaw led a gang of thieves who robbed banks and trains?

> Jesse Jackson
> Jesse James
> James Bond
> James Joyce

30. Supermarket products that are NOT brand names and usually cost less are known as what type of products?

> Genial
> Genuine
> Genetic
> Generic

31. Which worldwide organization wants to protect and save the environment?

Greenback Party
Greenwich Village
Greenpeace
Greenbelt Festival

32. Which of these things is NOT considered unlucky to do?

Open an umbrella inside the house
Walk near a ladder
Break a mirror
Let a black cat cross your path

33. Which of these is a fabric?

File
Cellophane
Corduroy
Plyboard

34. Which one below is NOT a sign of the zodiac?

Gemini
Capricorn
Pisces
Aquarium

35. Which of these things is considered a good luck sign?

T-bone
Collarbone
Wishbone
Crazy bone

36. Mark Twain is the pen name of:

Charles Lutwidge Dodgson
William Sydney Porter
Samuel Langhorne Clemens
Charles Lamb

37. Which of these terms is a synonym for "nothing"?

Nest egg
Candy egg
Scotch egg
Goose egg

38. Which thing is NOT worn around one's neck?

Petticoat
Lei
Collar
Scarf

39. What animal is known as a river horse?

Hippopotamus
Wolf
Elephant
Appaloosa

40. Which is NOT a volcano?

Mount St. Helen's
Mount Everest
Mauna Loa
Mount Etna

41. The main artery coming out
of the heart is the:

Amoeba
Anemone
Aorta
Anemia

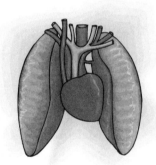

42. Which architect designed a private house known as
Fallingwater?

Michael Graves
I.M. Pei
Maya Lin
Frank Lloyd Wright

43. The ancient city of Constantinople is now called:

> Damascus
> Alexandria
> Istanbul
> Jerusalem

44. The South African policy of separating people by race is known as:

> Jim Crowism
> Apartheid
> Ghettoization
> Apathy

45. Which ingredient is NOT used to make s'mores over a campfire?

> Raisins
> Marshmallows
> Graham crackers
> Chocolate

(Answers are on page 81.)

Two for One

There are two clues given for each numbered item below; one word will answer both. Write it on the line provided.

Example: President George W. _____
      AND a landscaping shrub = _Bush_

1. Children's song "_____ Doodle"
AND a New York baseball player

_____

2. A famous cathedral in Paris
AND a university in Indiana (two words)

_____

3. Part of President Andrew Jackson's nickname
AND a type of nut

_____

4. Blues musician B.B. _____
AND the father of a prince

_____

5. Minnesota's football team
AND Scandinavian warriors

_____

6. Thomas Jefferson's mansion in Charlottesville, Virginia
AND a city in upstate New York

_____

7. Charlie Brown's dog
AND very nosy

_____

8. German composer Ludwig van _____
AND a movie (and sequels) about a St. Bernard dog

_____

9. Mission Impossible actor Tom _____
AND a pleasurable sea voyage

_____

10. Battleship nicknamed Old Ironsides
AND the written laws establishing the United States

_____

11. American Revolution hero who took that famous midnight ride, Paul _____
AND to honor and respect

_____

12. Pittsburgh baseball players
AND robbers at sea

_____

13. _____ Smith apple
AND the nickname for your Mom or Dad's mother

_____

14. Scientist/philosopher Francis _____
AND a popular breakfast meat

_____

15. Operetta by Gilbert and Sullivan HMS _____
AND a girl's sleeveless dress

_____

16. The longest river in the world
AND a shade of green

_____

17. A famous child actress of the 1930s and 1940s
AND a kid's drink from a restaurant bar (two words)

_____

18. Popular movie about a pig
AND baseball great _____ Ruth

_____

19. Common name for a lion
AND a sign of the Zodiac

_____

20. The fourth planet from the sun
AND scratches on a shiny surface

_____

21. President Ulysses S. _____
AND money often awarded to college students

_____

22. _____ Harbor, the site of a Japanese attack on America
AND a smooth lustrous gem

_____

23. The capital of Germany
AND White Christmas songwriter Irving _____

_____

24. Bees' homes
AND a skin problem with itchy red bumps

_____

25. Twenty-five-cent coins
AND living spaces

_____

26. Actress Jennifer _____ Hewitt
AND a tender feeling of affection

_____

27. Former Vice President Al _____
AND to stab with a sharp object

_____

28. Poet Robert _____
AND to put icing on a cake

_____

29. A famed 1954 Supreme Court case, _____ vs. the
Board of Education
AND the color of wood

_____

30. A shade of yellow
AND what the Indians called corn

_____

31. Alaskan fish that is often smoked
AND a shade of pink

_____

32. Asian country whose capital is Beijing
AND high quality dinnerware

_____

33. The twentieth President's last name
AND a famous lazy cartoon cat

_____

34. Our planet
AND soil

_____

35. The national bird of the United States
AND a type of Boy Scout

_____

36. City in Ohio
AND President Grover _____

_____

37. St. Louis baseball player
AND high-ranking Catholic Church official

_____

38. The largest Great Lake
AND way above average

_____

39. Frankfurter
AND the "nickname" of a dachshund (two words)

_____

40. Rapper whose birth name is Shad Moss
AND a sound made by a dog (two words)

_____

41. One branch of the Armed Forces of the U.S.
AND a shade of dark blue

_____

42. The name of a forest in Arizona
AND being so frightened that you cannot move

_____

43. Champion golfer _____ Woods
AND a large striped mammal

_____

44. Type of slip-on shoe
AND a lazy person

_____

45. A baby cow
AND a part of your leg

_____

46. Basketball player Michael _____
AND a country in the Middle East

_____

47. Traditional Thanksgiving food
AND the country whose capital is Ankara

_____

48. Person who shows a lot of courage
AND a kind of large sandwich

_____

49. Publisher Katharine _____ of _The Washington Post_
AND a type of cracker

_____

50. Painter _____ O'Keeffe
AND the state whose capital is Atlanta

_____

51. _____ Lake City, Utah
AND a common seasoning

_____

52. French general _____ Bonaparte
AND a custard filled pastry made of flaky layers

_____

53. The last name of the family in *Little Women*
AND the third month

_____

54. Mythological character who carried the world on his shoulders
AND a book of maps

_____

55. Explorer Christopher _____
AND a city in Ohio

_____

56. Metal used in thermometers
AND the planet closest to the sun

_____

57. The only mammal that flies
AND baseball equipment

_____

58. A German city with a famous cathedral
AND a scented liquid

_____

59. Roman goddess of love
AND tennis champion _____ Williams

_____

60. First woman Supreme Court Justice, Sandra ____
O'Connor
AND a 24-hour period

_____

61. City in South Carolina
AND dance popular in the Roaring Twenties

_____

62. The eleventh President, James _____ Polk
AND the location of the U.S. gold supply, Fort _____

_____

63. _____ Coast, a country in West Africa
AND the material that makes up an elephant's tusks

_____

64. Resort area of Massachusetts, _____ Cod
AND a sleeveless garment

_____

65. Baby kangaroo

AND nickname for Joseph

_____

66. Singer Britney _____

AND pointed weapons

_____

67. Baseball's first black player _____ Robinson

AND nickname of Mrs. John F. Kennedy

_____

68. Skateboarder Tony ____

AND a bird of prey

_____

69. Hong _____, a city in China

AND a famous movie about an ape, King _____

_____

70. _____ Express, a 2004 movie

AND a type of bear

_____

71. _____ Rouge, a city in Louisiana
AND a stick used by an orchestra conductor

_____

72. Founder of modern nursing Florence _____
AND a songbird

_____

73. Aviator _____ Earhart
AND a children's book character, _____ Bedelia

_____

74. Roman god of the sea
AND the eighth planet from the sun

_____

75. _____ Fe, New Mexico
AND _____ Claus

_____

(Answers are on pages 82–83.)

Relations

Beginnings

For this section, grab a scrap of paper and write in your answers. All the answers in each section BEGIN with the word in italics. Note: Some answers are not "real" words.

1. Name the *George* who:

__ was re-elected for a second term as President in 2004

__ was the first President of the U.S.

__ directed the Star Wars movies

2. Name the *Saint* that's:

__ a city in Missouri

__ a large strong dog

__ another name for Santa Claus

3. Name the *air* that's:

__ a jet

__ a system that keeps you cool in summer

__ a fast way to send letters to foreign places

4. Name the *baby* that's:

__ a person who watches children

__ a type of piano

__ a pastel color

5. Name the *belly* that's:

__also called a navel

__a really bad dive into a swimming pool

__a pain in your stomach

6. Name the *Bill* that's:

__the president of Microsoft

__a former President of the U.S.

__the term for the American Constitution's first ten amendments.

7. Name the *black* that's:

__a flying creature

__a classroom object for writing on with chalk

__a person who makes horseshoes

8. Name the *blue* that's:

__a casual item of clothing

__a small fruit

__an award for first place

__a mountain range in the Appalachians

9. Name the *cross* that's:

__a type of skiing

__a piece of sewing that forms an X

__a questioning by an attorney in a trial

10. Name the *paper* that's:

__a soft-covered book

__an item used to hold papers together

__a male who delivers newspapers

__a sack for holding groceries

11. Name the *yellow* that's:

__an infectious disease of warm climates

__a stinging wasp

__a telephone book that lists numbers and addresses
   of businesses

12. Name the *new* that's:

__a country near Australia

__another name for an infant

__a city in India

13. Name the *ten* that's:

__an apartment renter

__a type of cowboy hat

__a cut of beef

14. Name the *cat* that's:

__a short sleep

__a major religion of the world

__a treat for felines

15. Name the *bread* that's:

__a place to hold rye, white, and pumpernickel

__the person who supports a family

__an item used to cut a loaf

16. Name the *hard* that's:

__a type of egg

__something a construction worker wears for protection

__something that causes suffering

17. Name the *John* that's:

__an astronaut who became a senator

__a movie star of the past who was famous for his cowboy roles

__the musician who was known as "The March King"

18. Name the *dog* that's:

__a swimming stroke

__a type of tree

__another name for Sirius

19. Name the *double* that's:

__a spy who works for two enemy countries

__two baseball games held in the same session

__an illegal way to put your car on the street

__a cooking utensil with two nested pans

20. Name the *Jack* that's:

__a pop-up child's toy

__a cut-out pumpkin with facial features

__a type of dive

21. Name the *snow* that's:

__a small vehicle for traveling over snow

__something a baby wears in the winter

__a plant with round white flowers

22. Name the *sun* that's:

__a lotion people use at the beach

__an ice cream treat

__part of a car with a sliding panel

23. Name the *white* that's:

__rafting in river rapids

__a wave with a crest of foam

__the President's residence

__a discount event where household linens are offered
   at reduced prices

24. Name the *little* that's:

__a commercially sponsored baseball association

__nursery rhyme character who "lost her sheep"

__nursery rhyme character who "sat on a tuffet"

25. Name the *Mary* that's:

__ one of the Olsen twins

__ a painter whose works include many mother and
child scenes

__ one of the thirteen original colonies

26. Name the *four* that's:

__ a term for the typical family car

__ a term for a home run

__ a type of bed

27. Name the *show* that's:

__ a person who likes to attract attention to herself
or himself

__ an area where cars are displayed

__ an activity for young children where they talk about
something of interest to them

__ a catchy song from a musical production

28. Name the *two* that's:

__ a type of bathing suit

__ a type of bike

__ a type of highway

29. Name the *sand* that's:

___ a child's play area in a park

___ a mound found on the beach

___ a shoe usually worn in the summer

___ food made with two pieces of bread and a filling

30. Name the *day* that's:

___ a city in Florida

___ a city in Ohio

___ a place where children are supervised while their parents work

(Answers are on pages 83–85.)

Relations

Endings

Now get out a new sheet of paper and try these. All the answers in this section END with the word in italics.

1. Name the *stone* that's:

__the oldest national park

__a row house in an urban area

__an imitation diamond

2. Name the *house* that's:

__an outdoor dwelling for a pooch

__a place for growing plants

__an apartment on the highest floor of a building

__a storage place for merchandise

3. Name the *land* that's:

__the country whose capital is Bern

__the country whose capital is Helsinki

__the place Alice visited in a Lewis Carroll story

__the name of cities in Maine and Oregon

__the country whose capital is Edinburgh

__the country whose capital is Warsaw

__the type of jazz music that started in New Orleans

4. Name the *way* that's:

__the country next to Sweden

__a type of street that allows traffic in both directions

__the theater area in New York City

__the galaxy containing our solar system

5. Name the *moon* that's:

__a vacation for newlyweds

__the name of explorer Henry Hudson's ship

__an imaginary being that lives in the sky

6. Name the *party* that's:

__a sleepover

__an outdoor event that takes place among flowers and trees

__an event during the American Revolution

7. Name the *tower* that's:

__a tourist sight in Paris

__a place for observing takeoffs and landings at an airport

__a skyscraper in Chicago

8. Name the *ville* that's:

__a city in Spain

__a city in Tennessee

__a city in Florida

9. Name the *hood* that's:

__a lie

__a fairy-tale character who met a big bad wolf

__the period of a person's life from birth to about age 9

__a fictional outlaw who robbed from the rich to
help the poor

10. Name the *code* that's:

__used to dial a phone number

__used to make sure that no one is
wearing the wrong clothing

__a series of vertical lines on
all consumer products

11. Name the *stick* that's:

__used to eat food in a Chinese restaurant

__used by witches to travel

__a type of comedy that depends on gags, pie throwing,
and horseplay

12. Name the *phone* that's:

__worn when you're listening to a movie on an airplane

__used to amplify an emcee's voice so it can be heard
throughout a large area

__portable and is carried around in one's pocket or purse

13. Name the b*oard* that's:

__used for pressing clothes

__part of a bed

__used to jump into a pool

14. Name the *out* that's:

__a definition for a short break

__a synonym for exercise

__a situation where there is no electrical power

15. Name the *book* that's:

__a collection of recipes

__a synonym for purse

__an item with ruled pages used by students

16. Name the *case* that's:

__a place to hold a working person's papers

__a structure with steps

__an object that holds writing instruments

__a valise

17. Name the *more* that's:

__a place with four Presidents' faces carved into it

__the last name of actress Drew

__a second-year high school student

__a type of tree

18. Name the *market* that's:

__a place to buy used things very cheaply

__a large grocery store

__a place where professionals trade securities

19. Name the *call* that's:

__an attendance check

__an appearance by cast members at the end of a show

__a slang term for a mass audition of actors

20. Name the *card* that's:

__used by consumers instead of paying cash

__sent by many people in December

__a collectible item with pictures and statistics of major league players

21. Name the *neck* that's:

__a type of sweater

__a type of lamp

__a member of the U.S. Marine Corps

21. Name the *head* that's:

__part of the face

__a slang term for an intellectual

__an extinct volcano in Hawaii

22. Name the *well* that's:

__the last name of artist Norman

__a word that means good-bye

__a type of card sent to sick people

23. Name the *tape* that's:

__a type of parade where small pieces of paper are thrown out the window

__a term used to describe time-consuming bureaucratic procedures

__used in a VCR

24. Name the *can* that's:

__a colorful bird with a large beak

__the Roman god of fire

__a type of nut

25. Name the *mill* that's:

__used for grinding a popular seasoning

__an exercise machine for walking or running

__something the fictional character Don Quixote attacked, thinking it was a giant

26. Name the *row* that's:

__a small songbird

__the first name of President Wilson

__the day after today

27. Name the *rock* that's:

__ not really fake but is the national emblem of Ireland

__ the capital of Arkansas

__ where the Pilgrims stepped ashore in 1620 when they landed in America

28. Name the *roll* that's:

__ a list of names of people with high academic marks

__ an appetizer served in a Chinese restaurant

__ the total amount of money a company pays in wages

29. Name the *coat* that's:

__ a pretty slip worn by a girl

__ something worn when it's pouring

__ made of sable or mink

30. Name the *word* that's:

__ a secret term known by only a few people

__ a puzzle with Across and Down clues

__ a short introduction at the front of a book

(Answers are on pages 85–87.)

Singles

Art and Architecture

1. American Gothic, the painting by Grant Wood, shows a man and woman standing in front of a farmhouse. What object, which is associated both with the devil and with farming, is the man holding?

2. Which Spanish painter's most famous mural, Guernica, shows the horrors of war?

3. What North American country and its people were the subjects of most of Diego Rivera's paintings?

4. Pop artist Andy Warhol became an overnight sensation after painting what familiar canned food item?

5. Sculptor Auguste Rodin's most famous piece is of a man sitting down with his chin on his hand. What is the name of this sculpture?

6. What are the three primary colors?

7. Which Leonardo da Vinci painting of a smiling girl hangs in the Louvre Museum in Paris?

8. Agra, India, is the home of one of the most beautiful buildings in the world. What is its name?

9. Architect Frank Gehry designed an ultramodern concert hall in Los Angeles. For which well-known animator is it named?

10. I was born in Paris. I became a successful stockbroker, but I really wanted to be an artist. So I left my family and went to Tahiti and the Marquesas Islands to paint. My paintings now sell for millions of dollars. Who am I?

(Answers are on page 87.)

Cars

1. The Model T, produced by Ford between 1908 and 1927, came in only one color. What color was it?

2. What Michigan city is known as the Motor City?

3. What small Volkswagen model sounds like a bug?

4. What exam must people take before they can legally operate a car?

5. What term describes people having a picnic from the backs of their cars, usually before a sports event?

6. What racing event is held every year over the Memorial Day weekend?

7. Some cars combine two sources of power, like gasoline and batteries. What are such cars called?

8. The Aston Martin DB5 is associated with which film spy?

9. What is the name for a person whose job is to drive a car (usually for a rich person)?

10. What important manufacturing process did Henry Ford invent that made it possible to produce cars on a large scale?

11. What inflatable safety item protects drivers and passengers during an accident?

(Answers are on page 88.)

Critters

1. What animal part is used as a slang term for an antenna?

2. What fish sounds like a doctor who performs operations?

3. Which animal carries its "house" around with it and is the only animal that lives longer than humans?

4. What tiny creatures do aardvarks dine on?

5. These yellow weeds sound like fine jungle animals, but gardeners hate them and are always trying to get rid of them. What are they?

6. What are the two most common amphibians (animals that live both on land and in water)?

7. What do silk moths spin to protect their eggs?

8. These Australian critters live on eucalyptus leaves. What are they?

9. What is the tallest mammal?

10. Which animal can run as fast as 70 miles per hour?

11. Which bird drills through the bark of trees and has the same name as a cartoon character?

12. A male deer is a ___, a female deer is a ___, and a baby deer is a ___.

13. Name the famous collie that starred in movies and television.

14. What spotted dogs are frequently found at firehouses?

(Answers are on page 88.)

Days

1. Asian peoples celebrate this late winter holiday for 15 days, with parades, lion dances, and exploding firecrackers to ward off dragons. What holiday is it?

2. Which saint was given the name Maewyn Succat at birth and has a holiday named after him in March? What is the holiday?

3. On which holiday, celebrated on April 22, do people learn about ways to protect the environment?

4. What holiday, celebrated by dancing around a pole, is also an international labor holiday?

5. Which Canadian holiday that includes a festive meal is celebrated on the second Monday of October?

6. The city of Boston always holds a special event on Patriots' Day, which is celebrated on the third Monday in April. Name the event.

7. What summer month has no holidays at all?

8. Jews, Christians, and African-Americans celebrate three different end-of-year celebrations. Name each one.

9. In most parts of the United States clocks are set one hour ahead in April, starting a period called what?

10. On Veterans Day each year the President places a wreath at Arlington National Cemetery. On exactly whose memorial is this wreath placed?

(Answers are on page 88.)

Food

1. Which New England state is famous for its maple syrup?

2. What apple drink is popular in the autumn?

3. What veggie is used to make cole slaw and sauerkraut?

4. What fruit is related to a pumpkin and squash and is used mainly for decorations on Thanksgiving?

5. Cookies 'n Cream ice cream is made with what popular sandwich cookies?

6. Which plant has a thick reddish leafstalk and is often cooked with strawberries?

7. Cheese, milk, and yogurt are examples of what type of products?

8. What is the most important liquid you can drink to stay healthy?

9. This pulpy red food is actually a fruit but is most often used in salads. What is it?

10. What word goes in the blank space in this food riddle? "Did you hear the joke about the _____? I won't tell you because you might spread it!"

11. What green pulpy fruit is used to make guacamole, a popular item in Mexican cooking?

12. Pretzels, potato chips, cookies, candy, soda, etc., which are high in calories and low in nutrients, are known as what type of food?

13. What food do American children like most for lunch?

14. What breakfast dish is made with sliced bread soaked in a milk and egg batter and fried?

15. Cannelloni, fettuccine, and manicotti are examples of what kind of food?

16. What meat and vegetable dish is cooked slowly for several hours in a crock pot or on top of the stove?

17. Many kitchens have an item that holds small containers of basil, bay leaf, paprika, parsley, etc. What is this item called?

18. What fruit is most often used in an upside-down cake?

19. Gilroy, California, is known as the _____ capital of the world. What is this strong-smelling herb that is used in everything from spaghetti sauce to bagels?

20. This drink is made with milk, chocolate syrup, and seltzer, but not with the two ingredients that make up its name. What is it?

(Answers are on page 89.)

Geography

1. What is the capital of South Dakota? (Hint: It sounds like the name of a French boy.)

2. Hershey, Pennsylvania, is famous for manufacturing what product?

3. What New Jersey town was the location of a major battle in the Revolutionary War and is also home to an Ivy League university?

4. Which Missouri city is home to the Gateway Arch and the Museum of Westward Expansion?

5. Which Massachusetts city is nicknamed "Beantown"?

6. Which large Midwestern city suffered tremendous damage from the Great Fire in 1871?

7. Which Western city is home to many of the top companies in the U.S., including Microsoft Corp., Amazon.com, and Starbucks Coffee?

8. What is the name of Elvis Presley's mansion in Memphis, Tennessee?

9. What island near San Francisco operated a maximum security prison for 34 years?

10. Explorer Ponce de Leon, in search of the Fountain of Youth, landed in Florida near what present-day city?

11. Which continent is almost completely covered with ice?

12. Which section of Los Angeles is famous for its huge sign and its influence in the movie industry?

13. Which Rocky Mountain state is known for its potatoes?

14. In which country is the Great Wall located?

15. Kabul is the capital of which country?

16. Name the states that meet at the point known as the Four Corners.

17. The city of Dar es Salaam is located in what African country?

18. This city is the capital of the Czech Republic and is famous for the Charles Bridge and the ancient clock of the seasons. What is its name?

19. What is the name of the tiny country located in the mountains between France and Spain?

20. Name the country that is located at the southern tip of the second largest continent and whose cities include Cape Town and Pretoria.

21. Which Caribbean island is associated with cigars, Castro, and a 1962 missile crisis?

22. The Ginza district in Tokyo, with its neon lights and teeming crowds, is comparable to what district in New York City?

23. Oregon's nickname comes from that of a creature that constructs dams. What animal is it?

24. The nickname for the South is also the name of a famous paper cup maker. Name it.

25. Name a South American country that sounds like a spicy meat-and-bean dish.

26. Dover is the capital of which Eastern state?

27. Which suspension bridge is in San Francisco?

28. What flowery event takes place in Pasadena, California, each year on New Year's Day?

29. Which Southern city is associated with Mardi Gras, jazz music, jambalaya, and shrimp gumbo?

30. Which European city hosted the 2004 Summer Olympics and is famous for the Acropolis?

31. What is the name of the lost city of the Incas located in the Andes Mountains in Peru?

(Answers are on page 89.)

History

1. What was the name of the first Russian satellite, launched in 1957?

2. What family "relative" is popular as the symbol of the United States?

3. What New Deal program helped Americans save money for their retirement?

4. What's the name of the worst economic period in American history?

5. What gigantic ship hit an iceberg and sank on its maiden voyage in 1912?

6. What explosive weapon was dropped on Hiroshima, Japan, on August 6, 1945?

7. What was the name of the decade in U.S. history when flappers (women who wore short dresses) and speakeasies (places serving alcohol illegally) were very popular?

8. Which French palace, with its famous "Hall of Mirrors," was the setting for the signing of a treaty to end World War I on June 28, 1919?

9. Which South American leader helped his country gain independence from Spain in the early 1800s and what South American country was named for him?

10. In 1955, Rosa Parks' refusal to give up her bus seat to a white passenger sparked the Montgomery Bus Boycott by African-Americans. This was one of the first major events of what historical movement in U.S. history?

(Answers are on page 90.)

Kid Stuff

1. Who "kissed the girls and made them cry?"

2. In what dance do you "put your right foot in?"

3. In the nursery rhyme, what insect is told to "fly away, fly away, fly away home?"

4. In the playtime tune, what time of day do "we go 'round the mulberry bush?"

5. In the song "Oh, Dear! What Can the Matter Be," what hair decorations did Johnny promise to buy?

6. What pastries did the Queen of Hearts bake?

7. What fruit did Little Jack Horner pull out of his Christmas pie?

8. What was the "crown" that Jack broke when he fell down?

9. What small green item was placed under at least 20 mattresses to test if a princess was really a princess?

10. Which person "met a pieman going to the fair?"

11. What Dr. Seuss character stole Christmas?

12. The witch who captured Hansel and Gretel lived in a house made of what?

13. What are the words used to describe "Mary, Mary" who was asked "how does your garden grow?"

14. What appeared when Aladdin rubbed his magic lamp?

(Answers are on page 90.)

Literature

1. What word of affection is also the last name of Wendy, John, and Michael in *Peter Pan*?

2. What kind of Japanese poem is made up of three lines and 17 syllables?

3. Anne Frank was a Dutch Jewish girl who died in a concentration camp. What type of book did she write?

4. What famous horror tale was written by Mary Wollstonecraft Shelley?

5. Which German brothers, whose last name sounds stern, were the authors of Cinderella?

6. What fictional character, whose name is really two girls' names put together, always looks on the bright side of things?

7. I am the narrator of *The Catcher in the Rye*, one of the most famous novels of all time. What is my name?

8. My real name was Mary Anne Evans but my books were written under the name George Eliot. In one of my books, a weaver raises a child who is left on his doorstep. What is the name of this book?

9. E.B. White wrote a classic children's novel that includes such characters as Wilbur, Fern, and Templeton. What's the name of this book?

10. What inquisitive primate was created by H. A. Rey?

11. I am not your typical nanny. I take children on magical trips and I can talk to animals. Who am I?

12. This handsome youth in Greek mythology fell in love with his own reflection. What is his name, which is also the name of a delicate flower with white petals?

13. According to poet Carl Sandburg, what "comes on little cat feet?"

14. Who played a baseball game in Mudville in Ernest Lawrence Thayer's famous poem?

15. A simile is a figure of speech that compares two things using the words "like" or "as." Fill in the blanks for these common similes:

    a. sweet as _____
    b. proud as a _____
    c. cute as a _____
    d. smart as a _____
    e. quiet as a _____

16. When the orphan Mary Lennox goes to live with her uncle at Misselthwaite Manor, she is unhappy until she discovers a secret place. What kind of place is it?

17. Which author wrote *Treasure Island*, *Kidnapped*, and *The Strange Case of Dr. Jekyll and Mr. Hyde*?

18. Sir Arthur Conan Doyle's fictional detective lives at 221B Baker Street in London, England. Who is he?

19. I have only one name; I'm blind; and I'm known as the greatest storyteller in ancient Greece. Who am I?

20. Fill in the blank space with the word that completes this line by poet Joyce Kilmer:

> "I think that I shall never see
> A poem lovely as a ___."

(Answers are on page 90.)

Miscellaneous

1. During the Middle Ages, a peasant was regarded as property, just like the land he worked on. What was the word for this kind of peasant? (Hint: The word sounds like something you might do on the Internet or at a beach.)

2. A hogan is a Native American dwelling made of logs and mud. What Native American dwelling is made of skins or bark?

3. What natural disaster often destroys land and homes in California, Nevada, and Arizona in late summer?

4. What kind of test is given to determine if someone is telling the truth?

5. What nautical term is also a synonym for very neat?

6. Which zodiac sign is the sign of the twins?

7. What five-letter word means: an open space, a sports area, and a place of justice?

8. What part of your face is "out of joint" if you're annoyed?

9. You have probably never heard of Marion Donovan, but her 1951 invention freed mothers of newborns from having to do dirty laundry several times a week. What was this invention?

10. A numismatist collects coins and a philatelist collects stamps. What stuffed animals, named after a U.S. President, does an archtophile collect?

11. What did the Puritans call the "constitution" they drew up in 1620 after they arrived in the New World? (Hint: Put the boat that brought them to the New World with something a woman might carry in a cosmetic bag.)

12. The French franc, Spanish peseta, German mark, and other money were all replaced by what currency in 2002?

13. In 1967 the winner of the National Spelling Bee won first prize by correctly spelling "Chihuahua." What does this word mean?

14. What insect would you have "in your bonnet" if you are excited about something?

15. Words like "level" or phrases like "Madam, I'm Adam," which read the same forward and backward, are examples of _____.

16. When customers are buying something in record numbers, you would say the items were "selling like" what breakfast food?

17. What do you have to "face" when you suffer the consequences of your actions?

18. To do a job thoroughly, you must dot the ___ and cross the ___.

19. People who live in small apartments use a hideaway bed that can be folded into a closet. What is it called?

20. In 1967 John Shepherd-Barron invented a device that allows people to withdraw money from their bank accounts without going inside a bank. What is this device called? (Hint: It's known by its initials.)

(Answers are on page 91.)

Movies and TV

1. Christy Romano is the voice of what animated crime fighting character?

2. The film *Miracle on 34th Street* is about a girl who doesn't believe in what?

3. What is the name of Steven Spielberg's movie about a great white shark that terrorizes vacationers?

4. Which character with a bird's name on a kids' TV show has the ability to see the future?

5. Buzz Lightyear and Cowboy Woody are characters in what movie?

6. Mike Wazowski and Sulley team up in what kids' movie?

7. Name the clownfish who had to be found in a 2003 animated movie.

8. In a popular TV series, an orphaned girl lives with her adopted parents on a farm. Name the series.

9. Which TV series is about a family of four boys and their parents as seen through the eyes of the third oldest son?

10. What item does Tinky Winky, one of the Teletubbies, always carry on his arm?

11. Nala, Scar, and Mufasa are the names of characters in what animated film?

12. Which 2003 movie, starring Steve Martin and Hilary Duff, is about a very large family?

13. What TV series follows the Rugrats as they attend middle school?

14. In the 2004 movie *Shark Tale*, which actor/singer is the voice of Oscar?

15. What actor starred in the TV series *That '70s Show* and the movie *Dude, Where's My Car?*

(Answers are on page 91.)

Music

1. What famous '50s rock-and-roll star is idolized by Lilo in an animated movie?

2. Before he went solo, rock star Aaron Carter was part of a group whose name was the same as a street without an exit. What was it?

3. What "complicated" female pop singer was born in Canada and played hockey and baseball in school?

4. Which curly-headed 'N SYNC star was once known by the nickname "Brillo Pad?"

5. Which rapper is "in the money?"

6. Which hit CD *Game Time* rapper has a "lover"-ly name?

7. Which pop singer gets "the party started" and has a shocking head of hair?

8. The Italian composer, Antonio Vivaldi, wrote a series of concertos whose name sounds like calendar sections. What was it called?

9. Which female rocker sang "Everywhere" and "Are You Happy Now"?

10. Mick Jagger is the leader of which rock group?

11. What is the name for an organized group of singers who perform in a church?

12. What "colorful" rock band had the hits "Dark Side of the Moon" and "Comfortably Numb"?

13. His real name is Marshall Bruce Mathers III, but he goes by only one name. Who is this rap star?

14. Beyoncé, Kelly, and Michelle are the stars of what rock group?

15. Her hit songs include "Genie in a Bottle" and "What a Girl Wants." Who is this pop diva?

(Answers are on page 92.)

Numbers

1. True or false: By the year 2050, the world's population will be 8.9 billion.

2. At what age does a Jewish boy have his bar mitzvah?

3. 800, 866, and 877 are examples of what kind of phone numbers?

4. How many keys are on a piano keyboard?

5. How many innings are there in the normal baseball game?

6. What is the name of the puzzle where you make a picture by drawing a line from number to number?

7. The Roman numeral MCDXCII is what year in Arabic numerals? It is very significant in U.S. history.

8. What is the normal body temperature of a human (in degrees Fahrenheit)?

9. President Ulysses S. Grant is pictured on which United States bill?

10. When a married couple celebrates a silver anniversary, how long have they been married?

11. What five-digit (or sometimes nine-digit) number is placed at the end of an address?

12. What is the universal three-digit number for an emergency call?

13. A week has seven days and a month has 28, 30, or 31 days. How many days are in a fortnight?

14. Which four months have only 30 days?

15. When it's 2 a.m. on a Monday in New York City, what time and day is it in Los Angeles?

16. A girl in Latin America celebrates her quinceanera party at what age?

17. Triskaidekaphobia means fear of a number that is often associated with superstition and bad luck. What is this number?

18. All dinosaurs died out about _____ million years ago.

19. How many senators are there in the United States Senate?

20. What are the two numbers that you want to hear from your eye doctor because it means you have perfect vision?

(Answers are on page 92.)

People

1. Which comedian/actor was the voice of Shrek in the movie and sequel of the same name?

2. My name is Wilhelm Roentgen and I discovered the medical technology that allows doctors to see inside their patients. What is this technology called?

3. Which grandson of Queen Elizabeth of England will be king one day?

4. Which Civil Rights leader, who is honored on January 15th, spoke the words "I have a dream"?

5. Which "lucky" pilot flew the first nonstop flight from Long Island, New York, to Paris, France, in 1927?

6. Neil Armstrong's famous quote, "That's one small step for man, one giant leap for mankind," was in reference to what?

7. What Iraqi dictator was captured by American soldiers in 2003?

8. Which reporter won a Pulitzer Prize for his stories about the soldiers of World War II?

9. Which Soviet cosmonaut became the first human in space in 1961?

10. Which English film director, who was a master of suspense, directed the films *Psycho* and *The Birds*?

11. Who was the German goldsmith who invented printing with movable type? (Hint: His first book was a Bible.)

12. What is the last name of the three English sisters who wrote the novels *Jane Eyre*, *Wuthering Heights*, and *Agnes Grey?*

13. Name the woman who founded *Ms.* magazine and is still a leading force in the campaign for equal rights for women.

14. Who was the first female Prime Minister of Great Britain?

15. This African-American jazz singer was born in an orphanage and made her way to the top of the entertainment world. Her specialty was "scat" singing. She made up syllables and used her voice as an instrument. What is this singer's name?

16. Emma Lazarus' poem starts with this line: "Give me your tired, your poor, your huddled masses yearning to breathe free." At the foot of which symbol of freedom is this poem inscribed?

17. George Washington asked which Philadelphia seamstress to make the first American flag in 1776?

18. What Swiss hero shot an arrow through an apple on his son's head?

(Answers are on pages 92–93.)

Presidents and Their Families

1. Which U.S. President and founder of the University of Virginia was born on April 13, 1743?

2. Walt Whitman's poem, "O Captain! My Captain!" was written in memory of the death of which assassinated 19th-century President?

3. The highest mountain in North America is also the name of the 25th President of the U.S. What is it?

4. What are the names of the twin daughters of President and Mrs. George W. Bush?

5. What was the middle name of the sixth President of the United States, John Adams?

6. What is the address of the White House?

7. What music star/actress has the same first name as a former First Lady (although their names aren't spelled the same)?

8. November 22, 1963, was one of the saddest days in American history. What happened in Dallas that day?

9. Which 20th-century U.S. President, whose last name is the same as an American-made car, was born in Nebraska?

10. Who was the first President to visit China? The date was February 21, 1972.

11. The 34th President is often referred to by his initials, DDE, or by his nickname, Ike. What is his full name?

12. Who was the only U.S. President elected to four terms?

(Answers are on page 93.)

Puzzles and Games

1. In this game, a player chooses a word that must be guessed by another player. Each time there's a wrong guess, another part of a stick figure is drawn. What is the name of this game?

2. What game that is played in a swimming pool is named after an Italian explorer?

3. What card game, by its very name, is specifically meant to be played by only one person?

4. This game is often a child's first introduction to board games. It has sweet spots like Peanut Brittle House and Molasses Swamp. What is it?

5. This indoor game was popular centuries before radio and TV were invented. In the game, players act out words or phrases in pantomime to be guessed by other players. What is it called?

6. What strategy game requires two players to destroy each other's fleets of "war weapons?"

7. What game is played with nine squares and Xs and Os?

8. What do you call the space within a shopping mall where coin-operated games are found?

9. What electronic game has a character that eats its way through a maze?

10. What "toy" is really a small beanbag that is kicked around by kids?

11. What kind of puzzle uses pictures, letters, numbers, and symbols to represent words?

(Answers are on page 93.)

Science

1. Baby's breath is a small white flower that is often found in what type of bouquet?

2. On what part of your arm is the so-called crazy bone?

3. What antibiotic, discovered by accident by Alexander Fleming, was widely used to treat infections in soldiers during World War II?

4. What instrument used by doctors to listen to your heart was invented around 1819?

5. What serious disease can result from the bite of a dog that hasn't had its shots?

6. Where in Florida are manned space flights launched?

7. Marie and Pierre Curie were the husband-and-wife team who discovered which element?

8. Which New Zealand bird (which is also the name of a fruit) does not fly?

9. What body system contains the brain and spinal cord?

10. Animals such as kangaroos, opossums, and wombats carry their babies in pouches outside their bodies. What is the name for this order of animals?

11. A person who cannot distinguish between certain shades, like red and green, is said to be _____.

12. Some elementary classrooms contain a plastic case in which tiny creatures can be observed as they live. What is this item called?

13. Two distinctive star patterns within the constellation Ursa Major and its companion Ursa Minor are known by much more common names. What are they called?

14. What is the name of the phenomenon during which the moon casts a shadow on the Earth?

(Answers are on page 93.)

Sports

1. What symbols of peace are released at the start of every Summer Olympics?

2. What childhood game requires players to move like a rabbit through a numbered figure on the sidewalk?

3. The Iditarod starts in Anchorage, Alaska, and ends in Nome. What kind of race is it?

4. What three (very common) sports make up a triathlon?

5. What's the trademarked name for table tennis?

6. What term is used when a hockey or soccer player scores three goals in a game?

7. Who is the only person to win six championships in a row in the French bicycle race, the Tour de France?

8. The terms ollie and tabletop are associated with what city sport?

9. Birdie, bogey, and eagle are terms used in what sport?

10. What term of endearment means zero in tennis?

11. What professional sport does Tim Duncan play?

12. According to NFL history, two New Jersey colleges played the first football game in 1869. What are the names of these schools? (Hint: One is an Ivy League school and one is a state school.)

13. The Stanley Cup is associated with what professional sport?

14. Which Canadian city is home to major league baseball's Blue Jays?

15. In what sport do people wear masks and fight with swords?

16. What's the name of the place where relief baseball pitchers wait for their turn to pitch?

(Answers are on page 94.)

ANSWERS

Quadruples

1. Richter
2. Polio
3. Green Eggs and Ham
4. University of Southern California
5. Mississippi
6. Empire State Building
7. Xylophone
8. Cardinal
9. Brain
10. Sydney
11. Omega
12. Isaac Newton
13. Celery
14. Firedog
15. Jimmy Carter
16. A safe network to help slaves escape to freedom during the Civil War
17. A body of water between England and France
18. Gulliver
19. Venice
20. Lemony Snicket
21. Lakers
22. Plagiarism
23. Kielbasa
24. Touch and go
25. Spain and Portugal
26. P.T. Barnum
27. Charlie Chaplin
28. Water
29. Jesse James
30. Generic
31. Greenpeace
32. Walk near a ladder
33. Corduroy
34. Aquarium
35. Wishbone
36. Samuel Langhorne Clemens
37. Goose egg
38. Petticoat
39. Hippopotamus
40. Mount Everest
41. Aorta
42. Frank Lloyd Wright
43. Istanbul
44. Apartheid
45. Raisins

Two for One

1. Yankee
2. Notre Dame
3. Hickory
4. King
5. Vikings
6. Monticello
7. Snoopy
8. Beethoven
9. Cruise
10. Constitution
11. Revere
12. Pirates
13. Granny
14. Bacon
15. Pinafore
16. Nile
17. Shirley Temple
18. Babe
19. Leo
20. Mars
21. Grant
22. Pearl
23. Berlin
24. Hives
25. Quarters
26. Love
27. Gore
28. Frost
29. Brown
30. Maize
31. Salmon
32. China
33. Garfield
34. Earth
35. Eagle
36. Cleveland
37. Cardinal
38. Superior
39. Hot dog
40. Bow Wow
41. Navy
42. Petrified
43. Tiger
44. Loafer
45. Calf
46. Jordan
47. Turkey
48. Hero
49. Graham
50. Georgia
51. Salt
52. Napoleon
53. March
54. Atlas
55. Columbus
56. Mercury
57. Bat
58. Cologne

59. Venus
60. Day
61. Charleston
62. Knox
63. Ivory
64. Cape
65. Joey
66. Spears
67. Jackie

68. Hawk
69. Kong
70. Polar
71. Baton
72. Nightingale
73. Amelia
74. Neptune
75. Santa

Relations

Beginnings

1. George W. Bush
   George Washington
   George Lucas

2. Saint Louis
   Saint Bernard
   Saint Nicholas or
   Saint Nick

3. Airplane
   Air conditioning
   Airmail

4. Babysitter
   Baby grand
   Baby blue

5. Bellybutton
   Belly flop
   Bellyache

6. Bill Gates
   Bill Clinton
   Bill of Rights

7. Blackbird
   Blackboard
   Blacksmith

8. Blue jeans
   Blueberry
   Blue ribbon
   Blue Ridge

9. Cross country
   Cross-stitch
   Cross-examination

10. Paperback
    Paper clip
    Paperboy
    Paper bag

11. Yellow fever
    Yellow jacket
    Yellow Pages

12. New Zealand
    Newborn
    New Delhi

13. Tenant
    Ten-gallon
    Tenderloin

14. Catnap
    Catholic
    Catnip

15. Breadbox
    Breadwinner
    Bread knife

16. Hard-boiled
    Hardhat
    Hardship

17. John Glenn
    John Wayne
    John Philip Sousa

18. Dog paddle
    Dogwood
    Dog star

19. Double agent
    Doubleheader
    Double-park
    Double boiler

20. Jack-in-the-box
    Jack-o'-lantern
    Jackknife

21. Snowmobile
    Snowsuit
    Snowball

22. Sunscreen
    Sundae
    Sunroof

23. Whitewater
    Whitecap
    White House
    White sale

24. Little League
    Little Bo Peep
    Little Miss Muffet

25. Mary-Kate
    Mary Cassatt
    Maryland

26. Four-door sedan
    Four-bagger
    Four-poster

27. Show-off
    Showroom
    Show and tell
    Show tune

28. Two-piece
    Two-wheeler
    Two-lane

29. Sandbox
    Sand dune
    Sandal
    Sandwich

30. Daytona
    Dayton
    Daycare center

Relations

Endings

1. Yellowstone
   Brownstone
   Rhinestone

2. Doghouse
   Greenhouse
   Penthouse
   Warehouse

3. Switzerland
   Finland
   Wonderland
   Portland
   Scotland
   Poland
   Dixieland

4. Norway
   Two-way
   Broadway
   Milky Way

5. Honeymoon
   Half Moon
   Man in the moon

6. Slumber party or
      pajama party
   Garden party
   Boston Tea Party

7. Eiffel Tower
   Control tower
   Sears Tower

8. Seville
   Knoxville or Nashville
   Jacksonville

9. Falsehood
   Little Red Riding Hood
   Childhood
   Robin Hood

10. Area code
    Dress code
    Bar code

11. Chopstick
    Broomstick
    Slapstick

12. Headphone
    Microphone
    Cell phone

13. Ironing board
    Headboard or footboard
    Diving board

14. Time out
    Workout
    lackout

15. Cookbook
    Pocketbook
    Notebook

16. Briefcase
    Staircase
    Pencil case
    Suitcase

17. Mount Rushmore
    Barrymore
    Sophomore
    Sycamore

18. Flea market
    Supermarket
    Stock market

19. Roll call
    Curtain call
    Cattle call

20. Credit card
    Christmas card
    Baseball card

21. Turtleneck
    Gooseneck
    Leatherneck

22. Forehead
    Egghead
    Diamond Head

22. Rockwell
    Farewell
    Get well

23. Tickertape
    Red tape
    Videotape

24. Toucan
    Vulcan
    Pecan

25. Pepper mill
    Treadmill
    Windmill

26. Sparrow
    Woodrow
    Tomorrow

27. Shamrock
    Little Rock
    Plymouth Rock

28. Honor roll
    Egg roll
    Payroll

29. Petticoat
    Raincoat
    Fur coat

30. Password
    Crossword
    Foreword

Singles

Art and Architecture

1. A pitchfork
2. Pablo Picasso
3. Mexico
4. Campbell's Soup or
   Campbell's Tomato Soup
5. The Thinker
6. Red, yellow, blue
7. Mona Lisa
8. Taj Mahal
9. Walt Disney
10. Paul Gauguin

Cars

1. Black
2. Detroit
3. Beetle
4. A driving test
5. Tailgating
6. The Indy 500
7. Hybrid cars
8. James Bond
9. Chauffeur
10. The assembly line
11. Air bag

Critters

1. Rabbit ears
2. Sturgeon
3. Turtle or tortoise
4. Ants or termites
5. Dandelions
6. Frogs and toads
7. Cocoons
8. Koalas
9. Giraffe
10. Cheetah
11. Woodpecker (Woody Woodpecker)
12. Buck, doe, fawn
13. Lassie
14. Dalmatians

Days

1. Lunar New Year's
2. Saint Patrick; Saint Patrick's Day
3. Earth Day
4. May Day
5. Thanksgiving
6. The Boston Marathon
7. August
8. Hanukkah, Christmas, and Kwanza
9. Daylight savings time
10. On the Tomb of the Unknown Soldier

Food

1. Vermont
2. Cider
3. Cabbage
4. Gourd
5. Oreos
6. Rhubarb
7. Dairy
8. Water
9. Tomato
10. Butter
11. Avocado
12. Junk food
13. Peanut butter and jelly sandwich
14. French toast
15. Pasta
16. Stew
17. Spice rack
18. Pineapple
19. Garlic
20. Egg cream

Geography

1. Pierre
2. Chocolate
3. Princeton
4. St. Louis
5. Boston
6. Chicago
7. Seattle
8. Graceland
9. Alcatraz
10. St. Augustine
11. Antarctica
12. Hollywood
13. Idaho
14. China
15. Afghanistan
16. Arizona, Colorado, New Mexico, and Utah
17. Tanzania
18. Prague
19. Andorra
20. South Africa
21. Cuba
22. Times Square
23. Beaver
24. Dixie
25. Chile
26. Delaware
27. Golden Gate
28. The Tournament of Roses or the Rose Parade
29. New Orleans, Louisiana
30. Athens, Greece
31. Machu Picchu

History

1. Sputnik
2. Uncle Sam
3. Social Security
4. The Great Depression
5. *Titanic*
6. Atomic bomb
7. Roaring Twenties
8. Versailles
9. Simon Bolivar; Bolivia
10. The Civil Rights Movement

Kid Stuff

1. Georgie Porgie
2. The Hokey Pokey
3. A ladybug
4. Early in the morning (or morning)
5. A bunch of blue ribbons
6. Tarts
7. A plum
8. His head
9. A pea
10. Simple Simon
11. The Grinch
12. Gingerbread
13. Quite contrary or contrary
14. A genie

Literature

1. Darling
2. Haiku
3. Diary
4. *Frankenstein*
5. The Grimm Brothers
6. *Pollyanna*
7. Holden Caulfield
8. *Silas Marner*
9. *Charlotte's Web*
10. *Curious George*
11. *Mary Poppins*
12. Narcissus
13. The fog
14. Casey
15. a. honey
    b. peacock
    c. button
    d. whip
    e. mouse
16. A garden
17. Robert Louis Stevenson
18. Sherlock Holmes
19. Homer
20. Tree

Miscellaneous

1. Serf (surf)
2. Tepee or wigwam
3. Wildfires
4. Lie detector
5. Shipshape
6. Gemini
7. Court
8. Nose
9. Disposable diapers
10. Teddy bears
11. Mayflower Compact
12. The euro
13. A small Mexican dog
14. A bee
15. Palindromes
16. Hotcakes
17. The music
18. i's; t's
19. A Murphy bed
20. Automated Teller Machine or ATM

Movies and TV

1. Kim Possible
2. Santa Claus
3. *Jaws*
4. Raven from *That's So Raven*
5. *Toy Story*
6. *Monsters, Inc.*
7. Nemo
8. *Anne of Green Gables*
9. *Malcolm in the Middle*

10. A red purse, pocketbook, or handbag
11. *The Lion King*
12. *Cheaper by the Dozen*
13. *All Grown Up*
14. Will Smith
15. Ashton Kutcher

Music

1. Elvis Presley
2. Dead End
3. Avril Lavigne
4. Justin Timberlake
5. 50 Cent
6. Lil' Romeo
7. Pink
8. The Four Seasons
9. Michelle Branch
10. The Rolling Stones
11. Choir
12. Pink Floyd
13. Eminem
14. Destiny's Child
15. Christina Aguilera

Numbers

1. True
2. 13
3. Toll-free
4. 88
5. Nine
6. Dot-to-dot or connect the dots
7. 1492
8. 98.6 degrees
9. $50
10. 25 years
11. The ZIP code
12. 911
13. 14
14. April, June, September, and November
15. 11 p.m. Sunday
16. 15
17. 13
18. 65
19. 100
20. 20/20

People

1. Mike Myers
2. X-rays
3. Prince William
4. Martin Luther King, Jr.
5. Charles "Lucky" Lindbergh
6. The first moon landing on July 20, 1969
7. Saddam Hussein
8. Ernie Pyle
9. Yuri Gagarin
10. Alfred Hitchcock
11. Johannes Gutenberg
12. Bronte—Their first names were Charlotte, Emily, and Anne, respectively

13. Gloria Steinem
14. Margaret Thatcher
15. Ella Fitzgerald
16. The Statue of Liberty
17. Betsy Ross
18. William Tell

Presidents and Their Families

1. Thomas Jefferson
2. Abraham Lincoln
3. Mount McKinley
4. Jenna and Barbara
5. Quincy
6. 1600 Pennsylvania Avenue
7. Hilary Duff/Hillary Clinton
8. President John Fitzgerald Kennedy was assassinated.
9. Gerald Ford
10. Richard Nixon
11. Dwight David Eisenhower
12. Franklin Delano Roosevelt

Puzzles and Games

1. Hangman
2. Marco Polo
3. Solitaire
4. Candy Land
5. Charades
6. Battleship
7. Tic-tac-toe
8. Arcade
9. Pac-Man
10. Hacky Sack
11. A rebus

Science

1. Bridal
2. Elbow
3. Penicillin
4. Stethoscope
5. Rabies
6. Cape Canaveral
7. Radium
8. Kiwi
9. Central nervous system
10. Marsupials
11. Color-blind
12. Ant farm
13. The Big Dipper and the Little Dipper
14. Solar eclipse

Sports

1. White doves
2. Hopscotch
3. Dog sled race
4. Swimming, running, and bicycling
5. Ping-Pong™
6. Hat trick
7. Lance Armstrong
8. Skateboarding
9. Golf
10. Love
11. Basketball
12. Princeton and Rutgers
13. Ice hockey
14. Toronto
15. Fencing
16. The bullpen

Index

Art and Architecture, 46–47, *87*

Cars, 47–48, *88*

Critters, 49–50, *88*

Days, 50–51, *88*

Food, 52–54, *89*

Geography, 54–57, *89*

History, 58–59, *90*

Kid Stuff, 59–60, *90*

Literature, 61–63, *90*

Miscellaneous, 63–66, *91*

Movies and TV, 66–67, *91*

Music, 68–69, *92*

Numbers, 69–71, *92*

People, 72–74, *92–93*

Presidents and Their Families, 74–75, *93*

Puzzles and Games, 76–77, *93*

Quadruples, 7–18, *81*

Relations, 32–45,
  Beginnings, 32–38, *83–85*
  Endings, 39–45, *85–87*

Science, 77–79, *93*

Singles, 46–80, *87–94*

Sports, 79–80, *94*

Two for One, 19–31, *82–83*

WHAT IS MENSA?

Mensa
The High IQ Society

Mensa is the international society for people with a high IQ. We have more than 100,000 members in over 40 countries worldwide.

The society's aims are:
• to identify and foster human intelligence for the benefit of humanity;
• to encourage research in the nature, characteristics, and uses of intelligence;
• to provide a stimulating intellectual and social environment for its members.

Anyone with an IQ score in the top two percent of the population is eligible to become a member of Mensa—are you the "one in 50" we've been looking for?

Mensa membership offers an excellent range of benefits:
• Networking and social activities nationally and around the world;
• Special Interest Groups (hundreds of chances to pursue your hobbies and interests—from art to zoology!);
• Monthly International Journal, national magazines, and regional newsletters;
• Local meetings—from game challenges to food and drink;
• National and international weekend gatherings and conferences;
• Intellectually stimulating lectures and seminars;
• Access to the worldwide SIGHT network for travelers and hosts.

For more information about Mensa International:
www.mensa.org
Mensa International
15 The Ivories
6–8 Northampton Street
Islington, London N1 2HY
United Kingdom

For more information about American Mensa:
www.us.mensa.org
Telephone: (817) 607-0060
American Mensa Ltd.
1229 Corporate Drive West
Arlington, TX 76006-6103 USA

For more information about British Mensa (UK and Ireland):
www.mensa.org.uk
Telephone: +44 (0) 1902 772771
E-mail: enquiries@mensa.org.uk
British Mensa Ltd.
St. John's House
St. John's Square
Wolverhampton WV2 4AH
United Kingdom

For more information about Australian Mensa:
www.au.mensa.org
Telephone: +61 1902 260 594
E-mail: info@au.mensa.org
Australian Mensa Inc.
PO Box 212
Darlington WA 6070 Australia